THINK BETTER, WIN MORE!

How Sport Psychology Can Make You a Champion

Rob Gilbert, Ph.D.
and
Mike Tully

1st Edition. Rob Gilbert, Ph.D., and Mike Tully
Published by The Center for Sports Success
Bloomfield, NJ
Publishing date: April 2014
Originally published as "Gilbert on Greatness" (1988)

Disclaimer — Any improper or missing credits for the
stories and quotes contained in this book are unintentional.
The authors deeply regret any errors or omissions.

THINK BETTER, WIN MORE!

How Sport Psychology Can Make You a Champion

ROB GILBERT, Ph.D.
and
MIKE TULLY

A publication of
THE CENTER FOR SPORTS SUCCESS
91 Belleville Ave.
Suite 7
Bloomfield, NJ 07003
(973) 743-4428

Library of Congress
Catalogue Card Number

ISBN:

DEDICATIONS

To my mother and my father.
To my co-author, Coach Mike Tully — the smartest person
I know.
— Rob Gilbert

To my wife, Patty, my teammate for life. To mom and dad.
To my co-author, Rob Gilbert — a friend and mentor.
— Mike Tully

We are deeply indebted to:
Kirk Nicewonger for his editing.
Paola Morrongiello for the cover design.
Anthony Niebo for computer support.
Karin Abarbanel for her editing.

TABLE OF CONTENTS

How to Get the Most Out of This Book

This book is absolutely worthless ... if you just read it. This book is not meant just **TO BE READ** — it is meant **TO BE USED**. The techniques you will be introduced to here are useful only if you use them. They have been tested on thousands of athletes and hundreds of teams. And they work.

You can read this book any way you want: all at once or a little at a time. You can go from start to finish, or open to any page. No matter how you read it, there is something on every page to help you — if you **USE** it.

Write in the margins. Underline. Jot down notes in the pages at the end of the book.

If you find this book **THOUGHT-PROVOKING**, that's good.

But if you find it **ACTION-PROVOKING**, that's even better!

Remember, the **TECHNIQUES** work if **YOU** work them.

THE TEN MOST POWERFUL TWO-LETTER WORDS: IF IT IS TO BE IT IS UP TO ME.

CHAPTER 1

Your Introduction to Peak Performance

As an athlete, you spend a lot of time and effort getting your **body** in shape for competition — but how much time and effort do you spend getting your **mind** in shape?

Just as you train your body to increase your strength, to develop endurance and to perfect your skill, you also must train your mind so you will be able to relax, concentrate and be more motivated.

CONFUSED???

Well, let's make this a bit more personal ...

* Do you usually perform better in practice than in competition?
* Do anxiety, nervousness and panic keep you from doing your best?
* Have you ever performed so poorly in one event that discouragement lingered and you soon found yourself in a slump?
* Do certain opponents, teams, officials and even gyms psych you out?
* Do you often find yourself mechanically going through practice with little or no motivation?
* Do you spend a great deal of time worrying about what *might* go wrong?
* Do you always compete to win, or do you sometimes find yourself "playing it safe" so that you do not lose?
* Do you wish you had more self-confidence?

If you answered "yes" to even one of these questions, this book is for you. If you answered "yes" to more than one of these questions, this book is a *must* for you.

"MENTAL TOUGHNESS IS TO PHYSICAL AS FOUR IS TO ONE."
— *Bobby Knight*

CHAPTER 2

The Seven Key Mental Skills

Sport psychology has discovered something about you that has always been true —

WHAT YOU <u>THINK</u> AND HOW YOU <u>FEEL</u> AFFECT HOW WELL YOU WILL <u>PERFORM</u>.

Sport psychologists develop mental strategies and routines that can help you **do your best when it means the most**.

In other words, by training your mind *and* your body, you can learn how to do better than your best!

Often, the major obstacles athletes must confront to reach their full potential are mental. Let's look at some of the mental powers you will learn in this book:

The ability to relax: Are you able to fall asleep easily the night before a big competition and relax the day of the event so that you do not drain yourself of energy? The ability to relax will also help you overcome the feelings of fear and panic that happen just seconds before you perform.

The power of confidence: Even world-class athletes lose their confidence now and then. We'll show you how to build it day by day and to hold on to it.

The power of concentration: Do you keep your mind on what you are doing while you are doing it? This is the one master mental skill that the great athletes possess. Ever notice how great athletes are able to totally concentrate even though thousands of fans may be cheering?

How to get properly motivated: Peaking physically is not enough; you also need to peak mentally. You want to be psyched up and not psyched out. You must be motivated for practice as well as for competition. Legendary football coach Vince Lombardi said, "The will to win is not nearly as important as the will to *prepare* to win."

How to overcome the fear of failure: Competitions are challenges, not problems. As a matter of fact, the bigger the competition, the more you should look forward to it. After all, champion surfers go for the biggest waves and top-level mountain climbers seek out the highest peaks, don't they?

How to set goals: You would not take a trip without having a destination, but many athletes have no definite goals. The truth is, if you do not know where you are going, how are you ever going to get there?

How to go for it: After all is said and done, more is usually said than done. Taking action can turn your dreams into reality.

SUMMARY

Athletes who work on the mental aspects of their game start a very important process. They begin to realize how powerful the mind is. When you combine proper mental training with proper physical training every day, you develop your full capacities. When this starts happening, breakthroughs in your performances will not be far behind.

EVERYTHING YOU NEED
IS ALREADY INSIDE YOU.

CHAPTER 3

The Best Thing About Mental Training

Wow, you say. That's a lot to learn. Confidence ...
Relaxation ... Concentration ...

Well, here's some great news. You can train your mind
faster than you can train your muscles. A lot faster. Dr.
Gilbert proves it in his motivational talks.

Pulling a $100 bill from his wallet, he waves it in the air
and asks the audience, "Does anyone want this?"

No one moves, so Dr. Gilbert keeps waving the bill and
asking the question. Finally, someone gets out of their seat,
comes to the podium and timidly takes the bill.

A few minutes later, when Dr. Gilbert pulls another $100
from his wallet and waves it, no one hesitates.

No one in the audience has grown bigger, faster or stronger,
but they have been trained. It took just a few minutes.

And it can be the same way with you.

YOU CAN TRAIN YOUR MIND
A LOT FASTER
THAN YOU CAN TRAIN YOUR MUSCLES.

CHAPTER 4

One Skill You Can Improve Right Now

"Nothing can stop the man with the right mental attitude from achieving his goal; nothing on earth can help the man with the wrong mental attitude." — Thomas Jefferson

Let's say you have a game tomorrow.

What if you stayed up all night and worked out?

Would you get much stronger? **NO!**

Would you get much more skilled? **NO!**

Would you get faster, more agile, bigger? **NO! NO! NO!**

But there's something that you **CAN** change, and you can do it right now.

You can change your **attitude** about the upcoming competition.

"IT'S YOUR ATTITUDE, NOT YOUR APTITUDE, THAT DETERMINES YOUR ALTITUDE." — *Zig Ziglar*

CHAPTER 5

Think Better, Win More!

The way you talk to yourself can make all the difference in your mental state. A change in just one or two words can boost your energy and confidence.

First, if you're ever tempted to say you're **nervous,** use the word **excited** instead. Those butterflies in your stomach are nature's way of letting you know you're ready. Enjoy it. Hall of Fame baseball player Willie Mays said he had butterflies before every game of his career!

Second, if you're ever tempted to call any game **special,** call it **important** instead. Many years ago, Bill Clinton had a heart operation. Later, the head cardiac surgeon was asked what it was like operating on a former president. He said, "We knew it was President Clinton, but we treated him like any other patient."

In other words, this patient was important, not special.

**NERVOUS THOUGHTS BECOME
NERVOUS ACTIONS.
EXCITED THOUGHTS BECOME
EXCITED ACTIONS.**

CHAPTER 6

The Biggest Difference
Between Winners and Losers

The biggest difference between winners and losers is their attitude. The following story shows why.

Once upon a time, there were twin boys who at the age of 8 were driving their parents crazy because they were so different. One boy had a very negative attitude, while his twin was the exact opposite.

Their parents thought this to be very strange and took them to a psychologist. After meeting with the twins, the doctor asked them to come back in a week for a special session.

When the family returned a week later, the psychologist took the negative son down the hall and opened the door to a big room filled with rocking horses, video games and even ice cream, candy and cake. The psychologist said, "Why don't you stay here for a half-hour while I meet with your brother?"

Then he took the positive boy upstairs to a big gymnasium, where there was a big pile of horse manure. The psychologist said, "Why don't you stay here for a half-hour while I meet with your brother?"

When the psychologist went to check on the negative boy, he found him sitting in the corner and looking upset.

"What in the world are you doing," he asked the boy.

"I'm bored," came the reply.

"Bored? Why don't you play with the rocking horse?"

"I might fall off and get hurt," said the boy.

"Why don't you play the video games?"

"I don't know how."

"Why don't you have some ice cream, candy or cake?"

"I might get sick," the boy said.

"Well, follow me," the psychologist said, shaking his head in disbelief. They went upstairs to the gym, where they found the positive boy running excitedly around the pile of horse manure.

"What in the world are you doing," the psychologist asked.

The boy stopped, looked around and said, "With all this horse manure around, I figured there must be a pony here somewhere!"

NEGATIVE PEOPLE CAN BE GIVEN THE BEST OF CIRCUMSTANCES AND MAKE THE WORST OF THEM, WHILE POSITIVE PEOPLE CAN BE GIVEN THE WORST OF CIRCUMSTANCES AND MAKE THE BEST OF THEM.

CHAPTER 7

How to Develop a Winning Attitude

Attitudes grow by choice, not chance. You can choose to grow a winning attitude. You do it by picking the thoughts you put into your mind. These thoughts develop and shape your attitude.

When you start a garden and you plant carrots, you will get carrots. If you plant peas, you will get peas. But if you plant carrots, don't expect to get peas — you will get carrots. And if you plant peas, don't expect to get carrots — you will get peas.

It's the same with your mind. If you plant positive thoughts, you will grow a positive, winning attitude. If you plant negative thoughts, you will get a negative, losing attitude. Some athletes get upset because they plant negative thoughts and they expect to get a positive attitude. It doesn't work that way.

It is your choice: positive or negative thoughts. Positive attitude or negative attitude. Remember: A positive attitude is the key to success.

NOTHING POSITIVE WILL COME FROM BEING NEGATIVE, AND NOTHING NEGATIVE WILL COME FROM BEING POSITIVE.

CHAPTER 8

Turning Stress into Strength

* Do you ever feel terrified?
* Do you perform better in practice than in competition?
* Do you ever feel "out of it" just seconds before competing?
* Do you have trouble falling asleep the night before you compete?

If you have these or similar complaints, the cause may be excessive and/or uncontrolled stress. Mental training for athletes begins with the skills necessary to combat stress.

THE PROBLEM — STRESS

Actors call it stage fright. Teachers refer to it as test anxiety. Athletes experience it as anything from "butterflies in the stomach" to being "scared to death." No matter what you call it or how you experience it, you can deal with each of these forms of tension through relaxation training.

THE SOLUTION — RELAXATION

Let's start with three important assumptions:

Assumption No. 1: Circumstances, places and opponents do not make you tense — *you* make yourself tense. It is not what is happening to you but how you *respond* to what is happening to you that determines your level of tension.

$$E + R = O$$
Event Plus Response Equals Outcome
It's not the event that makes you tense. It's your response to the event that will make all the difference in the world.

Assumption No. 2: Since you cause your nervous tension, you can also cause yourself to relax. You are in control.

Assumption No. 3: You already know how to relax. You fall asleep every night, don't you? There is a natural tranquilizer inside of you that you can learn to use anytime you need it.

THE TECHNIQUE

The following eight-part technique will teach you how to relax naturally and effortlessly:

1. Find a quiet place where you will not be disturbed or interrupted for 15 to 20 minutes.
2. Sit comfortably in a chair. Have your legs uncrossed and your feet flat on the floor. Put your palms face down on your knees or thighs. Close your eyes.
3. Get in touch with your breathing. Consciously inhale, and exhale even more slowly.
4. Link your breathing with an image. As you inhale, imagine a big, beautiful wave coming in and crashing. As you exhale, imagine this wave going back out to sea. Keep the waves coordinated with your breathing, and your breathing coordinated with the waves.
5. Use all of your senses. See/feel/hear/taste/smell the waves. Ever notice how you can get totally involved in a movie? How you can laugh, cry or get very scared? You also have the inner ability to get totally involved with this calm, relaxing movie that you can show yourself in your mind.

6. Give the experience meaning. Just as the waves bring clean, fresh water to the shore and after they crash take any debris out to sea, as you inhale, realize that you are bringing fresh, relaxing energy into your body. As you exhale, feel that you are allowing any physical tension, upsetting thoughts and/or distressing emotions to leave.
7. Allow yourself to get totally into the experience. Get into the same state of mind as when you vividly daydream. Make the experience as real as possible.
8. After 12 to 15 minutes (you might want to use a timer), bring yourself back to the present. Do this slowly and gently, and bring all the nice feelings, thoughts and sensations that you might have experienced during the relaxation session back to the present.

STUMBLING BLOCKS

We have taught this relaxation technique to thousands of athletes. These are the most common stumbling blocks to successfully using this technique:

1. **"I can't make myself relax."** Correct. You cannot *make* yourself relax. In fact, the harder you try to *make* yourself relax, the more difficult it usually becomes. The secret is not to *make* it happen, but to *let* it happen. Let the natural process that your body already knows take over. Ever notice how you do not *make* yourself breathe, you *let* yourself breathe? You can learn to effortlessly let yourself relax.
2. **"It does not work."** Correct. The technique does not work — *you* work the technique. Like a new physical skill, a new mental skill will be developed only if it is practiced. All skills, both physical and mental, need practice and persistence to be refined.

3. **"I can't relax."** If you are alive, you know how to relax. What you might mean is, "I can't relax when I am under a lot of stress." You have the natural tranquilizers already inside you. You can do it. The solution: Apply the techniques found in this chapter.
4. **"I don't have enough time."** If you are too busy to relax, you are too busy. You will experience dramatic improvements and breakthroughs when you train your body *and* your mind.

CAUTION

This technique is not meant to be used immediately before practice or right before you compete. Practice this technique at an appropriate time every day. Late in the afternoon or early in the evening is a good time. If you have problems falling asleep at night, you can use this technique when you are in bed.

SUMMARY

Here is a relaxation technique that works. When you learn to apply this technique to stressful situations, you will begin to tap the power of your mind. As you keep doing this, you will be able to turn stress into strength, anxiety into excitement and problems into challenges.

WITH ENOUGH PRACTICE OF RELAXATION TECHNIQUES, YOU CAN TURN YOUR STRESS INTO STRENGTH WHENEVER YOU WANT.

CHAPTER 9

How to Think Like a Champion

Great athletes know how to think as well as play. Their mental skills and strategies are available to you. This chapter will give you enough information to start your own mental training program.

WHAT IS MENTAL TRAINING?

Your mind must be conditioned to withstand the stresses of your sport. You will play only as well as your mind lets you. This means that every day you must train your mind as well as your body.

WHY DOES IT WORK?

To tap the vast power of your mind, you must understand this important principle:

It is possible to deeply relax and imagine so vividly that for short periods of time *your mind and body do not know the difference between what is real and what is vividly imagined.*

For example, have you ever awakened from a nightmare in a cold sweat, with your heart racing? You might even have been screaming. Your mind and body were reacting as if the nightmare, this vividly imagined incident, were real.

For the same reason, when you vividly imagine yourself performing a skill perfectly, your brain sends out signals so that, without any apparent movement, your muscles are being trained in that skill and your brain is storing information as if it actually happened.

HOW TO GET STARTED

The technique that is used for mental practice is called imagery, and your mental training area is your imagination. Your imagination is already extremely powerful. You have been using it your whole life, and you have been strengthening it through dreaming, daydreaming, fantasizing and imagining. The secret of mental training is to focus on reviewing your positive experiences of the past and previewing your positive expectations of the future.

Suggestion: Use the following instructions to develop your own mental training CD. Speak in a slow, relaxed manner and leave enough time between the instructions so your mind can review and preview the appropriate experiences.

1. Allow yourself to relax.
2. Go back into your past and remember a time when you were extremely successful. Completely relive this experience. See what you saw ... feel what you felt ... hear what you heard. Whoever was with you then is with you again.
3. Go back into the past and recall a time when you performed extremely well. Allow yourself to get totally into this experience. See it ... feel it ... hear it.
4. Just as you have been reviewing events of the past, now just as vividly preview events of the future.
5. Imagine yourself at practice tomorrow, and see yourself doing little things better than you did before.
6. Imagine yourself as the athlete you want to be one week from now. Notice the improvement ... feel the confidence ... hear the approval of others.

7. Imagine yourself as the athlete you want to be one month from now. See what you want to see ... feel what you want to feel ... hear what you want to hear.
8. Now imagine yourself as the athlete you want to be one year from now. See yourself in practice and in competition. Notice that you are bigger, faster, stronger and more skilled.
9. Now imagine yourself reaching your ultimate athletic goal. Allow the experience to become as real as possible. Enjoy it.
10. Slowly allow all these experiences to fade out. Gently and effortlessly come back to the present time and place. Bring all of the positive feelings, pleasant thoughts and all the good physical sensations you might have had during this session back to the present.
11. Give yourself a few minutes to get reoriented. Open your eyes.

Use your mental training CD once a day. Speak slowly enough and leave enough time between instructions so that the CD is between 15 and 20 minutes long. The best time to listen depends on your schedule. Many athletes like to listen when they are in bed at night.

When you start to train yourself mentally, you will be amazed with the results.

C + B = A
Conceive Plus Believe Equals Achieve

WHAT YOU CONCEIVE IN YOUR MIND AND BELIEVE IN YOUR HEART YOU WILL ACHIEVE IN REALITY.
(Paraphrasing Napoleon Hill)

CHAPTER 10

The Magic of Thinking Bigger

Athletes make one big mistake when they set goals: **They aim too low**.

An example of this small thinking happened after one of Dr. Gilbert's lectures. An excellent college baseball player had several questions about goal-setting, and Dr. Gilbert asked him what his ultimate athletic goal was.

"I want to be a pro ballplayer," he said proudly.

"That's your ultimate goal?" Dr. Gilbert challenged him.

"I've wanted to be a pro ballplayer ever since I was in Little League," he said, smiling.

"Do you want to ride a bus for five months in the Florida State League?"

"No, of course not. I want to be a big-league ballplayer."

"Well, why didn't you say that? The lowest level minor-leaguer and the major-leaguer are both pro ballplayers."

Here's the point: If you want to be a big-league player, you should aim for the Hall of Fame. If you want to be a national champion, aim to be a world champion.

You're probably saying to yourself, "That's ridiculous. That's unrealistic."

Is it? There's the story of two insurance salesmen. One New Year's Day they decided to set goals for how much money they wanted to make for that year. One man wrote the figure $100,000 on an index card and sealed it in an envelope. The other man wrote down $1,000,000. A year later they opened the envelopes. The man who predicted $100,000 was ecstatic. "I hit my goal right on the mark," he exclaimed. His friend looked down at his card and said, "I guess I made it only halfway to my goal."

The man who *did not* reach his goal made five times the salary of the man who reached his goal!

At Williams College in Massachusetts, there is a plaque that reads:

Aim high, aim far
Your goal the sky
Your aim the stars.

If you want to reach the sky, you had better aim for the stars. In other words, the **bigger** goal you have, the **better**. Big goals produce excitement and enthusiasm. Could you imagine a 600-pound person getting excited about going on a diet to lose just 10 pounds in the next year? If he planned to lose 410 pounds, that would cause some excitement!

SUMMARY

Athletes too often set their goals too low. One of the biggest secrets of success is to set your goals outrageously high. Do not just aim, aim higher. Do not think big, think bigger.

"IF YOU DON'T DREAM BIG DREAMS FOR YOURSELF, WHO WILL?"
— Bill Parcells

CHAPTER 11

Changing Your Goal for Competition

What's your objective when you play?

If you said "to win," think again.

Your objective in every game should be to give a full effort.

Here's why:

When you focus on *effort*, you get more *success*. No matter what happens, your goal is full effort.

When you focus on *victory*, you get more *stress*. When the breaks go against you or when you fall behind, the anxiety mounts. Then you're in trouble.

World-class performers got where they are by giving a full effort.

Gandhi said, "Full effort is full victory."

Psychologists call this "Process over product."

The *product* is the final score.

The *process* is all the things that go into the final score: the effort, the attitude, the skills, etc.

PROCESS BEATS PRODUCT
EVERY SINGLE TIME.

CHAPTER 12

Goal-Setting Your Way to Success

"Setting goals is the first step in turning the invisible into the visible." — Tony Robbins

"Go for it!" "Make it happen!" "How much do you want it?" You will never get **it** until you know what **it** is.

The first step in any athletic activity is the formation of specific goals. After all, you would not take a trip without knowing where you are going, but many athletes go through their careers without goals. It is as simple as this:

**IF YOU ARE HEADED NOWHERE,
YOU MIGHT WIND UP
WHERE YOU ARE HEADED.**

THE POWER OF GOAL-SETTING

Human beings are naturally goal-directed. Whether it is food, shelter, money or status symbols, we always want to fulfill our wants, needs and dreams. As you direct and focus your attention on specific, meaningful goals, you unleash your inner power. More important, as your commitment to these things builds, you will start to tap into what Russian sport psychologists term "your hidden reserves" — the physical, mental and emotional resources that you have but **seldom use**. It is these hidden reserves that are responsible for peak athletic performance.

THE PROCESS OF GOAL-SETTING

While most athletes do not formally set goals, they all have dreams. Once you take these dreams and turn them into specific goals, you move closer to success. **Think of yourself as the architect.** What are you designing? Is it an ordinary structure or something incredibly striking? The following rules can help give you a solid foundation on which you can build your athletic skyscraper.

1. **Write your goals down.** Dreams are in your mind. Goals are written down on paper.
2. **Make your goals personal.** Goals are most meaningful when they are what you want for yourself.
3. **State your goals in the positive.** Concentrate on what you want most — not on what you want to avoid. "I want to win this match" is much more powerful than "I do not want to lose."
4. **Make your goals ideal but real**. For a goal to be effective, it must be believable.
5. **Think big**. The bigger the goal, the more motivating it becomes.
6. **Challenge yourself**. With your potential, the sky is the limit. Robert Browning said, "... a man's reach should exceed his grasp."
7. **State your goals as specifically as possible**.
8. **Give each goal a specific completion date**.
9. **Do it now!** Answer the questions in the next section to begin your personal goal-setting plan.

YOUR PERSONAL GOAL-SETTING PLAN

Get a pen or pencil and answer the following questions. Make sure that you follow the nine rules listed above, as they will help you to define your goals most effectively.

Keep this information confidential. Your goals will motivate only *you*. Do not impress teammates with your goals — impress them with your actions and progress.

This is a serious exercise. Do not just read this. Write down your answers.

1. What is your ultimate athletic goal? To become an Olympic gold medalist? A well-paid professional? An NCAA champion? A state champion? Whatever your dream is — write it down. By when do you want to reach this goal? Put down a specific completion date.

Ultimate Athletic Goal:

_____
_____
_____
_____

Completion Date:

_____

2. What do you want to accomplish in your sport in the next two to three years? These are your **Long-Term Goals**. What championships do you want to win? What awards do you want to receive? What teams do you want to make? List all these on a separate piece of paper. Now pick the three most exciting. Write them down here.

Long-Term Goal No. 1:

_____
_____
_____
_____

Completion Date:

_____

Long-Term Goal No. 2:

_____
_____
_____
_____

Completion Date:

_____

Long-Term Goal No. 3:

_____
_____
_____
_____

Completion Date:

_____

3. Think of what you want to become, everything you want to do and all the things you want to gain from your athletic career within the next year. Now pick the five that are most exciting. These are your **One-Year Goals**. Give each a specific completion date.

One-Year Goal No. 1:

_____
_____
_____
_____

Completion Date:

_____

One-Year Goal No. 2:

_____

_____

_____

_____

Completion Date:

_____

One-Year Goal No. 3:

_____

_____

_____

_____

Completion Date:

_____

One-Year Goal No. 4:

_____

_____

_____

_____

Completion Date:

_____

One-Year Goal No. 5:

_____

_____

_____

_____

Completion Date:

_____

4. **30-Day Goals**. What can you do in the next 30 days that will help you to accomplish your **One-Year Goals?** What skills do you need to develop? What weaknesses do you have to correct? What experiences can give you the competitive edge? Write all these down.

In the next 30 days, I will:

_____

_____

_____

_____

NOTE: Every 30 days, update this list.

5. What can you do **today** that will lead you one step closer to your **30-Day Goals**? Do you have to lift, run, practice, diet? Write it down.

Today I Will:

_____

_____

_____

_____

Caution: On any journey, you take either a direct or indirect route. This is true in goal-setting. Accomplishing your daily goals will take you one step closer to the attainment of your 30-day goals. When you accomplish your 30-day goals, it will lead you down the road to your One-Year and Long-Term goals. Does this road lead you to your Ultimate Athletic Goal? Have you plotted the most direct route? If not, make corrections. Take one step at a time. But first make sure that you are headed in the right direction.

GOALS AS MOTIVATIONAL TOOLS

Goal-setting can be your most important self-motivational tool. When you commit yourself to the accomplishment of your daily goals and you follow through on your commitment (your promises to yourself), you begin to trust yourself more. You will feel more in control. It adds up to more self-confidence.

This all starts one day at a time. Author John Bytheway said, "Inch by inch, life's a cinch."

You cannot do anything in the future. You can only do things in the present. Plan your future goals and do your daily ones.

When you commit yourself to your goals and you begin to see results, you will activate **the one most important force** that will propel you toward your ultimate athletic goal: enthusiasm.

"A JOURNEY OF A THOUSAND MILES BEGINS WITH A SINGLE STEP."
— *Lao Tzu*

CHAPTER 13

Are You Psyched Up or Psyched Out?

Most athletes never come close to reaching their potential because they fail to develop a tremendously important skill. This is not a physical skill — it is a mental one. Specifically, it has to do with your attitude as you go into competition. Dr. William James, the father of American psychology, wrote, *"It is our attitude at the beginning of a difficult undertaking which, more than anything else, will determine our success or failure."*

First of all, what is this thing called attitude? It is the sum of your thoughts and feelings at any one time about any one thing. You can allow your attitudes to vary greatly depending on your circumstances. It is as simple as this: Do you look forward to competing? Is competition an exciting challenge or a huge problem?

Let us explain, by way of the following example:

Have you ever noticed the difference in your attitude when you compete against an opponent you have defeated often (Situation 1) as opposed to your attitude when you compete against an opponent who has consistently beaten you (Situation 2)? For most athletes, Situation 1 brings feelings that are positive and excited, whereas Situation 2 leaves most athletes feeling negative and anxious.

Generally, most athletes in Situation 1 would have positive expectations or a winning feeling, while in Situation 2 they would have negative expectations or a losing feeling.

The skill is to have a winning attitude **regardless** of whom your opponent is.

DO NOT LET YOUR OPPONENT STEAL YOUR MENTAL AND EMOTIONAL INTENSITY.

Your opponent can do this only with your consent. It is not the opponent who causes your attitude to shift, but how **you choose** to respond to that opponent. In the end, **you are in control**. You determine whether you are psyched up or psyched out.

The problem with choosing to have a negative attitude is that you end up competing against yourself as well as your opponent. If you do not have the proper attitude for competition, there is only one person who will benefit: your opponent.

"WHETHER YOU THINK YOU CAN OR THINK YOU CAN'T — YOU ARE RIGHT."
— Henry Ford

CHAPTER 14

The Secret to Athletic Improvement

Do you want to be a better athlete? Do you want to make significant improvements that will greatly increase your chances of becoming a champion? Keep reading. In this chapter, you will learn a specific technique for doing better than your best.

To dramatically improve your performance, you must do two important things. First you need to work *harder* than you ever have. Second, you must work *smarter* than ever.

HOW TO WORK HARDER

You already know what you must do to work harder: Lift more ... run more ... learn more ... practice more ... compete more ... etc.

It is the same old story:

THE MORE YOU PUT INTO IT, THE MORE YOU WILL GET OUT OF IT.

HOW TO WORK SMARTER

All good athletes work hard. However, it is the great ones who also know how to work smarter. To discover the key to doing that, answer the following question:

Question: There are four steel rings. One can hold a maximum of 80 pounds. The second can hold no more than

60. The third can hold 40 and the fourth 20. If any of the rings must support more than its maximum, it will break. If all four rings are linked to form a chain, what is the greatest amount of weight that the entire chain can support?

a. 200 lbs.   b. 100 lbs.   c. 80 lbs.   d. 20 lbs.

Hint: *A chain is only as strong as its weakest link.*

Answer: d. 20 lbs.

Before you start to think that this chapter has more to do with the SATs than with sports, let's explain. The point is that the only way to strengthen the entire chain is to strengthen its **weakest** link. The maximum amount of weight the chain will hold will always be *limited* by its weakest link. As an athlete, you will always be limited most by your weaknesses. The smartest way for you to improve is to strengthen your weakest link.

Obvious? Sure. But isn't it human nature to practice the things that you do well and to ignore what you dislike or the thing at which you're not very good? The general rule is that if you want to make significant improvements in your skill, **spend more time strengthening your weaknesses than you do improving your strengths**. Once you do that, you will be working smarter.

HOW MUCH TIME YOU PUT IN IS NOT NEARLY AS IMPORTANT AS WHAT YOU PUT INTO THE TIME.

CHAPTER 15

The Power of the Present

"Yesterday is history.
Tomorrow is a mystery.
Today is a gift.
That's why they call it the present."
— Bil Keane

In this chapter, you will learn one of the most powerful techniques in sport psychology. This technique can dramatically raise your level of performance.

It can be summed up with these three powerful words:

DO IT NOW!

Right now is the only time in which you can ***make things happen.*** You can think about yesterday but you cannot do anything that changes what happened then. You can plan for tomorrow but you cannot do anything *until* tomorrow. You can make something happen only in this moment.

The power of the present comes from paying full attention to what you're doing. This ability to fully concentrate is one of the master skills of peak performers.

Rule No. 1: While you are practicing or competing, you will get superior results if your mind is on what you are doing ***while you are doing it.***

THE TECHNIQUE

Is this technique difficult? No. You keep your mind in the present much of the time. It's easy to do when you enjoy what you are doing. You are totally in the present when you watch a movie you really like. You are into it. The same thing happens when you are very interested in a book, a conversation, a class or a television show.

However, it is also very easy for your mind to slip out of the present. This usually happens when you are in situations that you perceive as stressful or boring. When your mind leaves the present, it goes to one of two places: the past or the future.

Rule No. 2: Fantasizing about the future or reminiscing about the past will not help you perform better in the present.

Example No. 1: It is a few minutes before you compete. You start worrying about losing, getting hurt, the score, etc.

Analysis: Your mind is **not** in the present. Your thoughts are in the future, about what **might** happen as the result of poor performance. This produces a tug-of-war between your mind and body. Your body is about to perform in the present while your mind is in the future. In this case you are not likely to do your best.

Solution: The thing **not** to do is to try to figure out **why** you are thinking like this. The thing to do is to get your mind back into the present.

Example No. 2: Your competition is about to begin. You remember how poorly you performed the last time you faced this opponent.

Analysis: Your mind is in the past. You cannot change what happened the last time you faced this opponent but you can do your best this time. Keep your mind in the present.

In both of these examples, the chance the athlete will choke is increased by worry over what might happen in the future or regret over what has already happened. Keep your mind in the present.

HOW TO DO IT

1. Become **aware** of whether your mind is in the present, past or future.
2. If you find that your thoughts are in the past or the future, **control** them and bring them back to the present.
3. **Practice** this skill in other situations. Classes and meetings are excellent opportunities.

WARNING

Use of this technique **does not** mean you should stop planning and setting goals for the future. It **does not** mean you should stop reviewing and learning from the past. Both of these activities are desirable, but not while you are performing.

SUMMARY

While you are practicing, **practice**. When you are competing, **compete**. Do it, body and mind together. **Do it now!!!**

DO WHAT YOU ARE DOING WHILE YOU ARE DOING IT.

CHAPTER 16

Snapping Your Way Back to the Present

Are you ready to do a little experiment with your mind? All you need is a thick rubber band. Put the rubber band around your left wrist. With your right hand, pull the rubber band back enough so it snaps against your wrist. What happens? You probably feel some discomfort, or maybe even a little pain. But, more important, what happens to your mind? Your mind snaps, too. Your mind snaps right back to the present.

Many athletes, singers, musicians, even comedians, use this technique. When your mind is all over the place and you can't focus, it's amazing how discomfort and pain snap your mind back to the present. Now, be careful. We don't want you to get a big monster rubber band that's going to cut off circulation to your arm! Just get something that will circle your hand like a bracelet.

Whenever you're sitting in class and you're not paying attention, snap your magic band. Whenever you're doing a homework assignment and your mind is wandering, snap your magic band. Whenever you're driving a car and (we hope this never happens) you're paying attention to anything other than driving, remember your magic band. After a while, you won't need the band. Just the thought of it will snap your mind back to the present.

DON'T DO 25 PUSHUPS.
DO ONE PUSHUP 25 TIMES.

CHAPTER 17

Winning Is Not the Only Thing

Here's a conversation between a wrestler and Dr. Gilbert.

Wrestler: One thing that drives me crazy is losing.

Gilbert: What do you mean?

Wrestler: I hate to lose.

Gilbert: What happens when you lose?

Wrestler: When I lose, I hate myself. I hate wrestling. I feel like quitting the sport.

Gilbert: Could you ever imagine that you could benefit from a loss?

Wrestler: No. Never. Losing is worse than dying because I have to live with losing.

Gilbert: So winning is the only thing?

Wrestler: Right.

Gilbert: You've never felt good after a loss, even if you wrestled well?

Wrestler: Never.

Gilbert: What if you were selected to represent your country in the Olympics? Just suppose the other wrestler was a three-time defending world champion. You wrestled a great match but lost in the closing second by one point. How would you feel?

Wrestler: Awful.

Gilbert: Why?

Wrestler: Because a loss is a loss.

This conversation actually took place. As a matter of fact, Dr. Gilbert has had similar conversations with many athletes who actually believe that **winning is the only thing.**

HOW TO WIN EVERY COMPETITION YOU ENTER

If winning is the most important thing, would you like to know how you can win all the time for the rest of your career? Here is the secret: **Compete only against those whom you are 100 percent certain you can beat.** The answer is a letdown, isn't it? It's a letdown because there is no excitement or thrill without a challenge. Going against opponents whom you are certain to beat offers no challenge. **Maybe winning is NOT the only thing**.

Suppose you're a surfer. Would the thrill come from repeatedly practicing on the safe, little waves or from going after the big ones? If you were a mountain climber, would you be satisfied climbing little hills or would you want to scale the great peaks?

As an athlete, do you seek out an easy level? If you are on the varsity, do you plead with the coach to put you in the JV lineup so that you can defeat less-skilled opponents? Of course not. The challenge and thrill come from trying to become the best you can be. **Maybe winning is NOT the only thing**.

44

WHAT ROCKY CAN TEACH YOU
ABOUT WINNING

Rocky Balboa, the Italian Stallion in the Rocky movies, is one of the greatest symbols of winning in our culture's history. He does not defeat every opponent, but he takes every challenge and never loses his spirit.

This spirit makes Rocky an excellent role model for athletes. He teaches us that winning is not the only thing. In the first Rocky film, Rocky lost and still felt like a winner because he went the distance with Apollo. That shows us that great challenges spur us to new heights. In "Rocky IV" he came out of retirement to fight — not for the money but for the challenge.

Most of all, Rocky teaches us that winning is not about whether you have defeated your opponent but whether you have maintained your winning attitude ... regardless of the outcome. The thing people love about Rocky is not his record but his winning attitude. You may lose a match but never lose your winning attitude.

WINNING IS NOT THE ONLY THING, BUT KEEPING A WINNING ATTITUDE — ALL THE TIME — IS EVERYTHING.

CHAPTER 18

Your One Most Important Fan

On your road to athletic success, you need the support of fans. Have you ever noticed that the more success teams and individuals achieve, the more of a following they tend to develop? However, you can have all the people in the stands cheering for you and it does not mean a thing — unless you are your own biggest fan. By "fan," we mean a person who cheers you on, a person who believes in you, a person who supports you in good times and bad.

Unfortunately, many athletes do not become their own best fans because they are their own worst enemies.

ARE YOU YOUR OWN WORST ENEMY?

There are several competitors who stand between you and any championship. However, your toughest opponent is always yourself. After all, who is the only person who can stop you from running tomorrow morning? Who is the only person who keeps you from working out more often? Who is the person who puts most of the pressure on you? Of course, the answer is **you**.

There is no harm in losing. In many cases, the real damage happens **after** the loss when athletes beat themselves up. Beating yourself up takes the form of subjecting yourself to severe self-criticism, developing a negative attitude, losing your self-confidence, going into a state of depression, etc. Who inflicts this punishment on you? Surely it was not your competition. We have known athletes who mentally tortured themselves for days, weeks and even months after a loss.

Look how harshly you can treat yourself. You would not let
a friend treat you as badly as you sometimes treat yourself.
You have enough opponents in sports without being your
own worst enemy.

HOW TO BECOME YOUR OWN BIGGEST FAN

If you want to become a champion, you have to become
your own biggest fan. All you have to do is be as committed
to yourself as you are to your best friend **and** to learn to like
yourself as much as your best friends like you. The two
important skills that you can learn from your friendships are
commitment and self-acceptance.

COMMITMENT

Our guess is that you are probably more committed to your
best friend than you are to yourself. Let us explain. How did
your relationship with your best friend become stronger?
Over the years, you proved yourself loyal, dependable and
trustworthy to this person by promising to do things and
then actually following through and doing them. You said
that you would help ... and you did. You said that you would
work out together ... and you did.

What happened when you consistently did not keep the
promises you made to a friend? Either your friendships
ended or your friends placed little trust in what you said
because they soon learned that what you said and what you
actually did were often two different things. In other words,
you did not keep your word.

The same holds true for the way you treat yourself. Are you
a good or a bad friend to yourself? Have you discovered
that what you say you will do and what you actually end up
doing are two different things? Do you keep your word to
yourself? When you promise yourself you will work out ...

do you? When you decide to go on a diet ... do you stick to it? When you set goals ... do you strive to achieve them? The result of keeping your word to yourself is improved **self-confidence**. The consequence of not keeping your word is increased **self-doubt.**

In order to be your own best friend, you have to be loyal, dependable and trustworthy to yourself. To do this, start keeping your commitments.

SELF-ACCEPTANCE

Ever notice that your best friends accept you exactly the way you are? They do not like you more if you win and they do not care for you less after you lose. Their friendship is not contingent on your performance as an athlete.

Are you this accepting of yourself? Many athletes feel they have to be **better than** someone else before they can feel good about themselves. The secret is: The better you feel about yourself, the better you will be able to deal with the emotional roller-coaster of sports. Many athletes get into a vicious cycle of always having to prove themselves. The cycle goes around and around until the athlete breaks the cycle — by burning out.

Fair weather fans are around only for the victory celebrations. True fans stay with their team through thick and thin. Don't be a fair weather fan — believe in yourself **all the time.**

IMAGINE IF YOU LIKED YOURSELF AS MUCH AS YOUR DOG LIKES YOU.

CHAPTER 19

The Secret That Champions Know

Once upon a time, there was a wrestler who wanted very much to be a champion. He had been competing for years but had never finished first. Oh sure, he had come close, but never placed better than second. Frustrated, discontented and upset, he wondered why he had lost so many close matches. He wondered what he had to do to become a champion. He ran, lifted weights, went to summer camps ... yet did not excel.

It was at one of these close matches where he became most frustrated by his lack of progress. After getting upset by a weaker opponent, he felt on the verge of quitting. He packed his equipment and left the gym without even changing.

While going through the parking lot to his car, he saw a coach about whom he had heard great things. He was walking to the gym. This coach, now in his early 60s, was in his time a great champion.

The story goes that he would have been an Olympic gold medalist had he not suffered a severe injury. Now he was an extremely successful coach at a very small college where he was known for taking average high school athletes and turning them into collegiate champions.

The wrestler seemed to be automatically steered in the coach's direction. Without thinking, he approached the coach and blurted out, "Coach, you don't know me, but I need to talk with you."

"What can I do for you?" the coach asked.

"Well, I'm quitting the sport."

"Oh really. Why is that?"

"Well, I work hard but I do not get any results."

"Results? What do you mean by results," the older man asked.

"I mean I don't win any tournaments."

"Oh, those kind of results. Tell me, what would happen if you did win a tournament?"

"It would be great. I'd be so psyched. Even just having that medal around would make me feel like I accomplished something."

The coach paused and said, "I think I understand ... but let me tell you how I see your situation. I have been in this sport for a long time. I've known a lot of champions. Seen them develop. Known them for years. But even though there are a lot of individuals who compete in our sport, as far as I'm concerned, they all fall into one of two categories: the 98 percenters or the 2 percenters. The 2 percenters are the champions and the 98 percenters are everyone else."

"I guess I'm a 98 percenter," said the athlete, looking down.

"Not so quick," countered the coach. "The best-kept secret in our sport is the one that all the 2 percenters know and that none of the 98 percenters know. This secret is the reason that the 2 percenters become champions and the 98 percenters do not."

"What's the secret?" the wrestler pressed, now totally attentive.

"Well, it is very simple. You see, the 98 percenters keep waiting until they become champions before they will start acting like champions. The 2 percenters start acting like champions well before they actually become one."

"I'm not so sure I follow you," the athlete said.

"Let's look at it this way. Suppose I had the results of next year's championship right here," he said, lifting the newspaper he was carrying. "And just imagine that you saw your name listed as a national champ. Now let me ask you this. If you knew, beyond the shadow of a doubt, that this would definitely happen, how would you feel right now?"

"Fantastic. Absolutely fantastic," the wrestler replied.

"If you knew that would be the case," the coach continued, "how much more self-confidence would you have?"

"A whole lot more."

"Would an early-season loss bother you?"

"No, not that much," the wrestler said, showing more confidence.

"How much harder would you train?"

"I'd go all out."

"How much more committed would you be?"

"Forget it. I'd be so psyched."

"Now you're talking like a 2 percenter," the coach said.

"It reminds me of the story I always tell my athletes about the shivering young man and the pot-bellied stove. The man sits in front of the stove yelling, 'Give me heat. Give me heat. Then I'll chop the wood.' You see, the 98 percenters, like that young man, have it all backwards. First you have to think, feel and act like a champion and then you will become one."

The wrestler looked like a huge lightbulb went on in his head. "You mean **acting** like a champion would make it more likely that I would actually **become** one?"

"That's right. You got it. Having a strong belief that something is going to happen makes it more likely that you will do the things necessary to make it happen. A strong belief and, of course, a lot of hard work can produce what is called a self-fulfilling prophecy. Do you follow what I'm saying?"

"Yes, I do," the wrestler replied. "I really do."

They kept talking.

Then the wrestler said, "Let's go to the gym."

"ACT THE WAY YOU WANT TO BECOME AND YOU WILL BECOME THE WAY YOU ACT." — *Bob Dylan*

CHAPTER 20

Your Toughest Opponent

The toughest opponent you will ever face is yourself, and in particular, your own fear. An important part of your training is learning how to overcome this fear. In this chapter, Dr. Gilbert draws on some interviews he's done with some very special teachers. These teachers showed their students how to overcome fear. Their techniques will work for you.

TEDDY ATLAS

Teddy once was one of the country's top boxing trainers. He worked with many top fighters, including great heavyweight champion Mike Tyson. Dr. Gilbert asked Atlas how he taught his fighters to overcome fear. The trainer had a remarkable answer. He equated fighting with war and said that in war there are only two types of soldiers — the heroes and the cowards. In combat, both the hero and coward feel fear. The difference is not in **what they feel**, the difference is in **what they do**. The hero feels the fear and acts, while the coward feels the fear and stops. Courage is not the absence of fear but the ability to feel the fear and go for it anyway. Very simply, courage is a choice. When gripped with fear, heroes take action. Others don't. Be a hero.

TOLLY BURKAN

Tolly has taught thousands of people around the world to walk on fire. That's right. As a matter of fact, Dr. Gilbert took his course and graduated when he walked over hot coals estimated to be 1,200 degrees Fahrenheit. But Tolly says he is really in the business of teaching people how to overcome fear. According to Tolly, **FEAR** is an acronym for **F**alse **E**ducation **A**ppearing **R**eal. Fear is something we learn. Psychologists tell us that we are born with only two fears: the fear of falling from high places and the fear of loud noises. We are not born with a fear of snakes, a fear of public speaking or a fear of certain opponents. These fears are developed. So if you created and developed these fears, who do you think can overcome them? That's right, you!

As an athlete, what fears have you created and developed that now stop you? Take action against these fears. Be a little braver. Hall of Fame football coach Vince Lombardi said, "Fatigue makes cowards of us all." Legendary comedienne Lucille Ball said, "I'm not funny. What I am is brave."

When you feel fatigue, be a little braver. Run that next lap **all out** ... then, when you compete against that superstar, be a little braver. Look him or her straight in the eye, and go **all out**. Choose to be courageous. Be a hero.

"FEEL THE FEAR AND DO IT ANYWAY."
— *Susan Jeffers*

CHAPTER 21

Where All Success Begins

There is one quality that separates the superstar athlete from the rest of the competition. If you find this quality, your performance will improve instantly and dramatically.

It's a simple quality called passion. Maybe you've heard the Ralph Waldo Emerson quote, "Nothing great was ever accomplished without enthusiasm." This is what we're referring to — an absolute love of what you are doing.

If there's one athlete who shows this absolute love, it's surfer Bethany Hamilton. She loves surfing so much that she kept doing it even after a shark attack left her with only one arm. Not only did Hamilton return to surfing, she won two championships and finished in the top five in several other tournaments.

Baseball Hall of Famer Cal Ripken never played with a flashy style. Instead he showed his passion by how often he showed up. Ripken played in 2,632 consecutive games, breaking the previous record by more than 500! He loved his work so much that he showed up every day for 16 seasons.

Let's be more specific about what we mean by passion. It comes in three parts:

1. Love of your sport.

2. Love of yourself.

3. Love of the process.

Love of your sport. The great classical pianist Vladimir Horowitz comes to mind. Well into his 80s he was still performing to sellout crowds. When asked why he kept playing, Horowitz answered that he was always learning something new. He had an absolute fascination with the piano.

Unfortunately, most coaches know first- or second-year athletes who think that they know it all. Great performers are just the opposite. They know that sports, with all its subtleties and intricacies, always leaves more to learn. Coach Tully was once speaking with Dr. Carl McGown, a volleyball coach who has been part of seven Olympics. Seven! And he's won three gold medals. At the end of a long day in which everything seemed to be a struggle, Coach Tully said to Coach McGown, "I'm just trying to be a better coach." Answered McGown, "So am I."

Dr. Gilbert knows more motivational stories and quotes than anyone, but he never stops looking for more.

Like Horowitz, McGown and Gilbert, you can study your field for the rest of your life — and never know it all.

Love of yourself. Without a doubt, the one thing that holds athletes back — more than anything else — is low self-esteem. In other words, they do not love themselves enough. You can be your own best friend, your own biggest supporter, your most faithful fan. Unfortunately, many athletes never do this.

Let's ask a question: What do you like most about yourself? There is only one right answer — **everything**. That's right. Your strengths, your weaknesses, everything that makes you the unique person you are.

There is an incredible song by Whitney Houston titled "The Greatest Love of All" that conveys this message:

Learning to love yourself
It is the greatest love of all.

Love of the process. As an athlete you are on a constant roller-coaster. Enjoy the ride. You have to love the downs as well as the ups. True peak performers enjoy the process (the training, the practicing, the drilling, the bus rides, etc.) as well as the products (the winning, the trophies, the praise). Dr. Gilbert has always noticed that many high school stars quit sports during their freshman year of college. He thinks this is because once they get to college, they realize they have to start climbing the ladder to success all over again. It is as if they were back in the ninth grade. They left high school as heroes and now find themselves just another member of the team. Dr. Gilbert's interpretation is that those athletes do not love sports as much as they love winning. Since winning may not be immediately achievable, they quit. Don't be like this. Learn to love the process.

SUMMARY

There you have it: The one biggest secret of the superstars is passion.

One more important thing: The superstars did not become passionate because they were winners. They became winners because they were passionate. The passion came first, before the winning, and this is the secret that made them great.

WINNING DOES NOT LEAD TO PASSION; PASSION LEADS TO WINNING.

CHAPTER 22

How to Do the Impossible

Last week I turned 18 ...
I haven't done anything yet,
So I made this deal with myself.
This is the year I make my mark.
— Louden Swain in "VISION QUEST"

To become a champion you must do the impossible. You have to work out harder, lift more and run farther than you ever thought possible. You will have to beat opponents you consider to be unbeatable.

You can do it! The first step is to bury words like *can't*, *if* and *maybe*. Just rip these words out of the dictionary in your mind. Champions do not use these words.

The second step is to practice doing the impossible. That's right — practice. To get you started in the right direction, we're going to give you an assignment. It's called "The Impossible Challenge." It's mandatory but voluntary. It's mandatory because if you want to create breakthroughs in your athletic career, you have to do it. However, it's voluntary because it is up to you whether you actually complete it.

THE IMPOSSIBLE CHALLENGE

Within a week after reading this chapter, do something that you now consider impossible.

Let's look at the idea of impossible. Don't try to leap over tall buildings in a single bound, grow seven inches or levitate. Those are all truly impossible.

Instead, do things that **your mind** has said are impossible. For instance, an athlete once told Dr. Gilbert that it was impossible for her to run three miles every day — even though she was already running two miles a day. A wrestler said it was impossible to diet even for one day in the off-season. A gymnast reported that it was impossible for her to call a former friend with whom she had had an argument. Of course, in all three cases the athlete wound up doing what *their mind* had told them was impossible. After three miles, the runner discovered that the barrier was mental, not physical. The wrestler stayed on his diet for 24 hours. And the gymnast said that even though the call to the former friend was not an easy one to make, it led to the renewal of a friendship.

All found that doing the impossible was a matter of changing the way they **spoke to themselves** and **thought about themselves**. They stopped saying, "I can't," because "I can't" really means "I don't want to."

Become aware of the way you speak to yourself. See how often you say things like "I could never do that" or "That's impossible." When you talk to yourself in such negative terms, these words turn into the negative thoughts that fill your mind. When you constantly fill your mind with these negative thoughts, you are programming yourself for negative actions and negative results.

Look around you. You'll see other people who are doing things you think are impossible. If they are doing it, you can learn to do it, too!

WHY DO THE CHALLENGE?

In your life, you have done the impossible hundreds of times. Remember that summer at the pool when you kept looking at the high diving board, but knew it would be impossible for you to dive off it — even though others were doing it? What happened when you finally decided to dive, even though you were scared to death? When you went for it, when you jumped and lived, what did you spend the rest of the day (and summer) doing? That's right — diving off the high board.

When you do the impossible, you unleash an incredible amount of blocked-up energy. You turn **limited thoughts** into **limitless thoughts**.

Unfortunately, we block our energy and think limited thoughts too often. It's like we are driving a car with the emergency brake on or watering the lawn while standing on the hose. We work against ourselves. Once we stop doing this, once we change our limited thoughts, the impossible becomes possible. You can tap more of your unlimited potential by changing your thoughts.

When you complete The Impossible Challenge, write to us. Tell us exactly what you did and how you felt about doing it. When we hear from you, The Center for Sports Success will send an Award of Commendation that certifies you did the impossible. Once you do the impossible, nothing should stop you from doing it over and over.

REQUIRED VIEWING

To get a fuller understanding of The Impossible Challenge, see the movie "Vision Quest."

"NOTHING IS IMPOSSIBLE. THE WORD ITSELF SAYS, 'I'M POSSIBLE!'"
— *Audrey Hepburn*

For your certificate, send your letter to:

Dr. Rob Gilbert
The Center for Sports Success
91 Belleville Ave.
Suite 7
Bloomfield, NJ 07003

CHAPTER 23

The Power of Tremendous Teamwork

Is your team a **real team** or just a collection of athletes? There are very few real teams. There are many groups of athletes who work out and compete together but are a team **in name only**. There is an enormous difference between a group of athletes who **work out together** and a group of athletes who **work together**.

A team is a group of athletes who work together for a common goal, and not just a group of athletes who wear the same uniform.

From the lowest to the highest levels of sport, teams are filled with dissension, greed, envy, backstabbing, etc. If you want your team to become a real team, not just a collection of athletes, everyone on the team must start working together.

PULLING TOGETHER

Imagine that your team is in a tug-of-war. To win, every single member has to give an all-out effort in unison — **everyone pulling together**. There are three types of participants who will ruin your team's chances in a tug-of-war:

1. Participants who give an all-out effort but do not pull together with their teammates. In other words, they are doing their own thing. If they were soldiers, they would be out of step. If they were musicians, they would miss the beat.

2. Participants who hold onto the rope but do not pull. Such people are team members in name only. These are takers, not givers. They want all the privileges and take none of the responsibility.
3. Participants who pull in the opposite direction. These people work against their teammates and are poisoning the effort with dissension.

MORAL: TEAMS EITHER PULL TOGETHER OR PULL APART — THERE IS NO IN-BETWEEN.

REAL TEAMWORK

Dr. Gilbert gives talks and workshops to businesses as well as to athletic groups on how to develop teamwork. The participants are amazed when he tells them that great teamwork is more likely to be found in concert halls than on athletic fields. Let's explain.

Did you ever see a symphony orchestra? There can be more than 100 members. Some, like the concert master, have big parts, and others, like the person who crashes the cymbals, might perform only once all night. Nevertheless, for everyone to be "in concert," everyone has to play together.

If you want your team to be more of a well-oiled machine, learn from the great orchestras. Everyone plays together — everyone pulls together. It is a group effort.

WHY TEAMWORK WORKS

Every once in a while in the world of sports, we see great teamwork. Maybe you've heard of the 1980 U.S. Olympic hockey team. They won the gold medal by upsetting the

Soviet Union and the rest of the world in a sports miracle. There were no superstars on that U.S. team; however, this was a superstar team. The unit brought out the best in everyone. In other words, **the whole became greater than the sum of its parts**.

When everyone on a team starts working and pulling together, a conspiracy develops. Does that sound odd? The word "conspiracy" comes from two Latin words meaning "to breathe together." When a group starts working together, there is power and magic. That is why armies march in step. It projects power. When they cross a bridge, they must briefly stop their rhythm, otherwise the power of their left-right steps would break the bridge. That is real power!

Ever go to a rock concert? There is incredible magic when everyone is singing and swaying together. In the Bible, group power brought down the walls of Jericho.

**HOW YOU CAN BECOME
A SUPER TEAM PLAYER**

How can your team develop the amazing power and magic of teamwork? It all begins with you. Commit yourself to start working with your teammates rather than against them. Refuse to be *selfish*. Become more *selfless.* Give more of yourself to your teammates and your coaches. You can start this pulling-together process. When your team starts pulling together, everyone will benefit — except your opponents.

THE BEST TEAM DOES NOT WIN
AS OFTEN AS
THE TEAM THAT GETS ALONG BEST.

CHAPTER 24

The Coach Is Always Right

Every coach should have a sign on his or her desk that reads:

Rule No. 1: The coach is always right.
Rule No. 2: If the coach is wrong, re-read Rule No. 1.

In counseling athletes, we have dealt with many athlete-coach crises. Dr. Gilbert is usually able to solve these problems by convincing the athlete that the coach is always right.

If you want to reach your full potential as an athlete, you **have to believe** the coach is always right. And if your team is to reach its potential, all the athletes on your team have to believe the coach is always right.

Some athletic teams become the battlegrounds on which player/coach wars take place. Guess what? There are enough enemies and opponents out there without creating more on your team. You and your coach **must be** allies. You are on the same team. As a player, your job is to be fully supportive of your coach.

Let's explain. Is the coach always right? No, of course not. Anyone who has to make all the decisions about performance and people that a coach does cannot always be correct. However, it is not the job of the athlete to keep a scorecard on the coach's performance. Why? Because the more time and attention athletes put into evaluating the coach, the less time and effort they put into their own performance.

By way of analogy, suppose this were the opening night of a Broadway play and you were one of the performers. You are on stage playing your role. The critics are in the audience. Your job is to perform, and the critic's job is to evaluate. Your performance as an actor will suffer as soon as you start thinking like a critic.

It's the same thing with you as an athlete.

The effort you put into evaluating and criticizing your coach will take away from the energy you put into your own performance.

As an athlete, you can treat your coach in one of three ways. Which one describes you?

1. I act as if my coach is always right. I support my coach, win or lose. I do not participate in or condone gossip about my coach. No matter what happens, my coach can count on me. If I were the coach, *I definitely* **would want** *a player with my attitude on the team.*
2. The coach is never right. We have disagreements. I often question his/her judgement, especially with other players on the team. There is a wall between us, and do not expect me to break it down. If I were the coach, *I would* **not want** *a player with my attitude on the team.*
3. I am still sitting in judgement and weighing the evidence. Do I trust him/her? Do I like him/her? Will I go out on a limb for him/her? I will let you know when I reach my verdict. If I were the coach, *I* **would not want** *a player with my attitude on the team.*

Of these three positions, only one will lead to improved personal and team performance. To be anything but supportive of your coach will not be beneficial.

One reason there is so much conflict between players and coaches is that they see the same thing in completely different ways. Athletes have a limited perspective. Most athletes are self-centered, and their first priority is themselves. Their concerns are whether they will start, how much they will play, whether their friends and family will be at the game, their plans after the game, etc. Coaches do not think that way. They have to think about what is best for the team.

This is very evident in sports like wrestling or tennis. The athlete competes in just one match, while the coach competes in all of them. Just watch the bench during one of these events. The athlete's full attention is on the match, just as it should be. But the coach must be intensely involved everywhere.

What specific things can you do to improve your relationship with your coach?

1. Do not ask questions like, "Why aren't I playing more?" Instead, ask questions like, "What can I do to improve?"
2. No second-guessing. Anyone can be a Monday-morning quarterback — that is, the kind of person who says what *should* have happened. Regardless of the situation, act as if your coach made the best possible decision.
3. The question you should be asking most often is, "What can I do to help?"
4. Take full responsibility for yourself. If you want to help your coach, your team, yourself, then your job is to do your job. Make sure you are at practice on time. Make sure you know when the bus is leaving. Take care of your

equipment. Do not worry about anyone else until you have taken full responsibility for yourself.

5. Do not publicly criticize your coach. **EVER.** How would you like it if your coach publicly criticized you? It is amazing how often the Golden Rule applies. "Do unto others as you would have others do unto you." You and your coach will have enough critics once the season gets under way.

SUMMARY

Are you part of the problem or part of the solution? As a member of a team, you are either helping the team split apart (in which case you are part of the problem), or you are helping the team pull together (you are part of the solution). You and your team have enough opponents out there without having dissension and competition within the team. This pulling together starts with your own relationship with your coach. It is up to you to make sure it is a good one!

WHO IS RIGHT
IS NOT AS IMPORTANT AS
WHAT IS RIGHT.

CHAPTER 25

The Power of Commitment

Once upon a time there were a chicken and a pig who were very good friends. They lived in a town that was very poor. Many people had only one or two meals per day. The chicken wanted to help these people, so she approached her good friend the pig and said, "I have an idea how you and I could help these poor people get a good breakfast."

"What could we do?" asked the pig.

"Well," replied the chicken, "I could give the eggs I lay, and you could provide ham."

*"I understand," said the wise pig, "but what is just a **donation** for you is a **total commitment** for me."*

As an athlete, do you make donations or do you totally commit to your sport? There is a huge difference. If you are wondering why you are not improving and reaching your goals even though you are putting in time and effort, the missing ingredient may be your commitment.

WHAT IS COMMITMENT?

A commitment is a promise you keep no matter what.

You are very good at keeping some commitments you make. Maybe there's a TV show that you watch no matter what, or a CD you'll listen to no matter what.

The problem is not that you do not keep your commitments. The problem is which *commitments you decide to keep*.

For example, have you ever promised yourself that you would study or work out, only to find yourself watching your favorite TV show? True, you have kept one commitment, but you have ignored the ones that could really help.

A TYPICAL SCENARIO

You promise yourself that you are going on a diet. An important part of this plan is that you will not eat between meals. The first day your diet goes well — until 9:30 at night. You realize that there is cold pizza in the refrigerator ... and you love cold pizza. The little voice in your mind tells you things like, "You can start your diet tomorrow" or "It's only one little piece, and you need the carbohydrates for energy."

You are just about to take a slice and bite into it. **Note:** At this moment you are in a tug-of-war with yourself. Your body and mind are a battlefield of conflicting wants and desires. Part of you wants to keep the commitment to your training, while the other part wants you to give in.

All of a sudden, a magic genie appears and tells you that you can have a wish come true if you do not have that pizza. Instantly there is no conflict ... no tug-of-war ... no battlefield. You decide that you would much rather have your wish than the pizza. As soon as you make that decision, you are not working against yourself anymore.

This magic genie is your inner strength. Once you develop this inner strength to keep your commitments, it will be much easier to have all your wishes come true.

Every time you keep a commitment to yourself, your inner strength grows. Every time you do not, you get back into a tug-of-war that distracts you from your goals.

THE COMMITMENT CHALLENGE

Do you want to develop incredible inner strength? Find a commitment that is possible to do, but hard enough to challenge you. Perhaps it's doing a certain number of push-ups or sit-ups every day for the next 28 days. Do them every day, **no matter what**.

If you meet this challenge, you will be well on your way to a championship season because you will be developing your commitment muscles.

LOSERS MAKE PROMISES. WINNERS KEEP COMMITMENTS.

CHAPTER 26

The Questions We Hear Most Often

In workshops and lectures on sport psychology, each year we work with thousands of coaches and athletes. The following are questions we are asked most frequently.

Question: What if I'm just not mentally tough? Maybe I just don't have what it takes.

Answer: Wrong! Your mental game, like your physical game, is a combination of skills that can be developed with the proper training. Most athletes train only their bodies at practice. They miss out on lots of opportunities to get tougher mentally. Every practice offers a chance to learn how to handle problems, doubts, victories, defeats. At practice you can set goals, visualize success and work on keeping your mind in the present. Start looking carefully at practice, and notice all the things you can accomplish there.

Question: I worry a lot about what other people think of me. What should I do?

Answer: It is very normal to be concerned about what other people think of you. However, to succeed, it is important to realize that what others think of you is not nearly as important as what you think of yourself. Do not let the criticism and negativity of others erode your self-confidence and steal your dreams. People will come into and leave your life ... you will always be with you. Be your own biggest supporter and your own best friend.

Question: My goal is to make the Olympic team. My problem is that I spend a lot of time worrying that I will not.

Answer: It's great to have set such a big goal. However, all the worry in the world will not help you reach this goal. Stop worrying and start planning! Set a definite plan to make this dream come true. Set goals you want to reach in one year, in six months, in one month, and, most important, today. Now put this plan into action. Right now, you do not have any control over what might happen years from now; you can plan and carry out your goals for today.

Question: After a big loss or disappointing performance, I fall apart. What advice can you give me?

Answer: Adversity introduces an athlete to him or herself. One thing that separates the champions from everyone else is how they deal with setbacks like injuries and losses. As Olympic wrestling champion Jeff Blatnick said, "You have to learn how to lose before you will be able to learn how to win."

Question: How come I go to practice every day and I do not improve?

Answer: Practice does not make perfect. Just because you go to practice every day does not mean you will improve. For example, look at something you do often — sign your name. If you are like most people, your signature has not improved in the last year — even though you have written it hundreds of times. The point is that **just going through the motions is not enough.** If you want to improve, practice perfectly. Perfect practice means having your body and mind doing the same thing at the same time. When you are practicing, keep your mind on what you are doing while you are doing it. Do not have your body at practice while your mind is in the locker room.

Question: Why do I get so nervous before a big event?

Question: Why do I have such a negative attitude?

Question: Why do I have such a problem getting motivated?

Answer: In all three of these cases, knowing **why** you are nervous, negative or unmotivated will not change the situation. It is more important to ask the question **how**. How can I relax? How can I have a better attitude? How can I get motivated? Once you have the answers to these *how* questions, you will have techniques you can use to solve the problems. Winners ask how, losers ask why.

Question: What is your favorite quote?

Answer from Dr. Gilbert: Homer Barr, my college wrestling coach, kept this quote in his office:

THE WILL TO WIN
IS NOT NEARLY AS IMPORTANT AS
THE WILL TO PREPARE TO WIN.

Answer from Coach Tully:

SOME PEOPLE THINK THE BATTLE IS
AGAINST OTHERS. THE WINNER
UNDERSTANDS THE STRUGGLE
IS WITHIN THE SELF.

CHAPTER 27

The Five Biggest Mental Mistakes and How You Can Overcome Them

There are two ways to become a champion. The slow way is to learn from your own mistakes. A much faster way is to learn from other people's mistakes as well as from your own. Not only is it a lot less painful, but once you start doing this you will begin to make fewer mistakes.

We have noticed, in our work with athletes, that they commit the same errors again and again. This chapter will give you the chance to learn from their mistakes. Here are the five biggest mental mistakes athletes make and how you can overcome them.

MISTAKE NO. 1: HOLDING BACK

Holding back is the biggest mistake you can make in sports or in life. Think of all the things you could have accomplished if you had been able to put aside your doubts and just go for it! Instead, people play it safe, trying not to lose instead of trying to win.

MISTAKE NO. 2: GIVING YOURSELF TOO LITTLE CREDIT
and
MISTAKE NO. 3: GIVING YOUR OPPONENT TOO MUCH CREDIT

In 1969 Joe Namath went down in history with a single prediction. Even though his New York Jets were huge underdogs — 19 points — to the Baltimore Colts, Namath **GUARANTEED** his team would win the Super Bowl.

At the time, people thought he was crazy, arrogant, foolish, or all of the above. Then he backed up his guarantee. The Jets won in the biggest upset in Super Bowl history.

Asked later how he could have made such an outrageous guarantee, Namath had a simple answer.

"I knew we were as good as they were," he said, explaining he had known some of them and seen some of them play.

In other words, Namath didn't believe the odds, the newspapers or popular opinion. He didn't give too much credit to the Colts, or too little credit to his team.

He just gave an all-out effort. It's an incredible lesson for you. Leave all the outside things to other people. Keep things simple.

MISTAKE NO. 4: "TRYING"

Trying is lying. As Yoda said to Luke in "The Empire Strikes Back," "Do or do not. There is no try." You can't **try** to get to practice on time. You can't **try** to do your homework tonight. You can't **try** to finish this book. In all cases, you either do or you don't. When a friend says they will **try** to give you a ride to the airport, it's time to call a cab. Don't be a tryer — be a doer!

MISTAKE NO. 5: DOING WHAT IS EXPECTED

The secret of real success is very simple: Do more than expected. One of Dr. Gilbert's former students, Melissa Sapio, used this formula. She graduated from Montclair

State University with a perfect 4.0 average. She took 44 courses and she got 44 A's. When asked her secret, she said, "Whatever my professors asked me to do, I would do more than expected. If my math professor assigned problems 1, 3 and 5, I would do problems 1, 2, 3, 4 and 5."

Here's your assignment. Read the biography of any superstar athlete. We will **guarantee** that throughout their athletic career, they did more than expected.

Coach Tully tells his athletes, "In any situation, you can do the average, above average or below average. It's entirely up to you, and it has nothing to do with size, speed or strength." This applies to conditioning, drills, homework, picking up equipment, everything in your life.

Excellence isn't expected effort. Excellence is extra effort.

MISTAKE NO. 6: K - A = 0
Knowledge Minus Action Equals Zero

Wait a second. The title of this chapter was "The *Five* Biggest Mental Mistakes and How You Can Overcome Them." Why are we doing Mistake No. 6? Because we don't want to make Mistake No. 5 and do only what is expected. We want to do more than expected.

We hope you are learning from this book. You likely have gained some knowledge. But if you know what to do but don't do what you know, it's worthless.

For example, now you know the power of doing more than expected. Are you going to do it?

Now you know relaxation techniques. Are you going to practice them?

Now you know about setting goals. Will you do it? Knowing about setting goals and actually setting goals are two different things. Are you going to *talk the talk* or *walk the walk*?

EVERYONE MAKES MISTAKES. SOME PEOPLE GET DISCOURAGED AND DEFEATED BY THEM. WINNERS LEARN FROM THEM.

CHAPTER 28

One Athlete's Biggest Mistake

Dear Coach,

You probably do not remember me — and I'm glad. I ran cross-country for you more than 20 years ago. I was on the high school team in my freshman, sophomore and junior years. I quit at the beginning of my senior year — that's why I hope you do not remember me. I'm the guy who walked out on you and the team the day before the Springfield High meet back then.

You deserved better. You coached me for more than three years and even let me come to your summer camps for free. You were one of the few teachers in school who ever took a personal interest in me. And I blew it.

My senior year, I quit because I *thought* I was sick and tired of going to practice, watching my diet and running early in the morning. All I really wanted was to get a job, buy a car and hang out with my girlfriend.

Back then I thought that these were good *reasons* for quitting. Now I know they were just reasonable *excuses*.

When I was 17, the things I wanted to get out of cross-country were trophies, a letter sweater and my picture in the yearbook. I had no idea about the real gifts that the sport could give me.

I remember that you always said, "You learn English, math and history in the classroom, but you develop character out on the track." How right you were. What I wanted from running was the thrill of victory; what I needed to learn was how to deal with the agony of defeat. You see, I was one of those guys who always took the easy way out — when the going got tough, I bailed out.

Quitting cross-country was one in a long series of things that I started but did not finish. It became a predictable pattern in my life. After getting fired three times and divorced twice, I began to realize that what you get out of something is directly related to what you put into it.

Coach, you are probably wondering why I am writing to you. First of all, I sincerely want to thank you for all that you did for me.

Second, I want you to know that I made a big mistake more than 20 years ago. I cannot change that now. But if someday one of your runners walks into your office and tells you that he is going to quit, maybe you can show him this letter. Because it is not too late for him. He can change his mind right now.

One more thing. How did my senior year work out after I quit? It went from bad to worse. I quit my job after three months ... then I totaled my car ... and when I had no car or money, my girlfriend dumped me. We did not even go to the senior prom together.

I remember the quote that you had on your office wall:

WINNERS NEVER QUIT
AND QUITTERS NEVER WIN

It took me 20 years to learn that lesson.

Sincerely,

A guy who wishes he went for it.

"FIGHT THROUGH IT."
— Jerry Rice

CHAPTER 29

You Can Be a Superhero

There is a superman or superwoman inside you trying to escape. Each and every one of us has this superhero trapped inside.

Every once in a while, you hear about people who perform superhuman feats:

* The woman who lifts up a car to free her child trapped underneath.
* The athlete who smashes a record no one thought could be broken.
* The sick or injured person told by doctors that there is no hope, who proceeds to **fully** recover.

Your inner superhero is made up of amazing abilities you seldom, if ever, use. Very few people ever tap their potential. We marvel at the feats of such pros as LeBron James, Serena Williams and Peyton Manning. But they didn't get to the top automatically. *The important thing to realize is that superstars have not necessarily been blessed with more ability than anyone else. They are superstars because they tap into and use more of their ability.*

Some people think Michael Jordan is the greatest basketball player who ever lived. Did you know that when Jordan was young, he was not even the best player **in his own neighborhood**? Sure, he had the ability. He just had not tapped into it yet.

YOU HAVE SUPERSTAR ABILITY, TOO

Now it is your job to tap and use these "hidden reserves."
Just because you have not yet used these reserves does not
mean they do not exist. For example, suppose you owned
the world's most powerful computer. How helpful would it
be if you did not switch it on and learn how to use it?

Guess what? You do own the world's most powerful
computer. It is sitting right on top of your shoulders. It is
your brain. Unfortunately, most athletes do **not** switch on
this computer and learn how to use it.

Here are some people who did:

* Spud Webb, at a height of not quite 5-foot-7, reached the
  NBA. And he did not stop there. One year he won the
  slam-dunk competition against people more than a foot
  taller than he was!
* Jim Abbott pitched for four big-league baseball teams
  despite having only one hand. He won 87 games,
  including a no-hitter.
* Olympic gold medalist Jeff Blatnick defeated cancer as
  well as the rest of the world to win the Greco-Roman
  wrestling title in 1984.

THERE IS A SUPERHERO INSIDE YOU. YOU HAVE ABILITIES YOU NEVER DREAMED OF. YOU HAVE THE POTENTIAL TO BE MUCH MORE THAN YOU ARE.

CHAPTER 30

It's Courage That Counts

"Success is never final.
Failure is never fatal.
It is courage that counts."
— John Wooden

It was his last chance. He was a senior and his goal was to
make it to the state wrestling championships. He had to win
this match to get a fifth-place medal and reach his four-year
dream.

The match was over. He stood with his head down as the
referee raised his opponent's arm in victory. It was not even
close. He had lost 9-0. His high school wrestling career was
over. There would be no state tournament for him. Not now
— not ever. This was his last chance. And he blew it.

Walking off the mat, he heard the cheers. He thought they
were for his opponent. But the applause kept getting louder.
He looked up. All eyes were on him. The 800 fans who
packed the small high school gym were standing and
cheering **him**. They were giving **him** a standing ovation. He
was overwhelmed. The emotions of the moment became too
much for him to handle. He went down to one knee and
cried.

Wrestling is a difficult sport for anyone. It is even more
difficult when you are born without a left arm. And his right
arm, if you would call it that, was really just one-half an

arm. He had two fingers growing out of an elbow-length stump.

He remembered when he first went out for the team in the ninth grade. Even the kids on his *own team* called him a freak.

Sophomore year was not much better. More comments behind his back. Hurtful statements to his face. Nicknames from the stands that no one should ever hear. That season he won his first match — by forfeit. The opposing coach refused to let his boy wrestle "an invalid."

By junior year the young man had developed his own style. What a leg-wrestler he was becoming! He won almost as many matches as he lost.

And senior year, the greatest moment of his life came when the coach told the team he was elected one of the co-captains. He ended with 11 wins and eight losses. He might not have been a great wrestler, but he was surely a great competitor. He earned the right to represent his school on the mat.

And now his wrestling career was over. His opponent was hugging him. His coach and teammates were picking him up and putting him on their shoulders. He saw his mom in the stands crying. And dad was recording the whole thing. The fans were still on their feet cheering.

They were giving this "losing" wrestler a standing ovation because the one-armed wrestler had shown everyone:

WINNING IS NOT THE ONLY THING ...
COURAGE IS.

CHAPTER 31

How to Build Confidence

This is a story about a young girl who couldn't care less about what others would say or think about her.

Nobody thought she was the smartest fourth-grader. Nobody ever said that she was the most musical, the most athletic or the most artistic. But this little girl was the world's most confident fourth-grader. She thought she could do absolutely anything.

One day, the art teacher came into class and said, "Today you can paint, draw, or finger-paint anything you want."

The world's most confident fourth-grader shot her hand into the air and said, "Can I draw a picture of God?"

Through her chuckles, the teacher said, "Nobody's quite sure what God looks like."

With all the confidence in the world, the little girl said, "Oh, they will be when I'm done!"

NOW THAT'S A WINNING ATTITUDE!

You have to do what this little girl did.

Care a little less about what other people will think about you.

Care a little less about what other people will say about you.

Let's face it, if a little fourth-grader can do it — YOU CAN DO IT, TOO!!!

So instead of worrying what people will think and what people will say about you, do what the little fourth-grader did . . .

ACT CONFIDENT!

The secret is to be a good actor.

**JUST BECAUSE YOU ARE WORRIED
DOESN'T MEAN
YOU HAVE TO ACT WORRIED.**

Another way of saying this is . . .

**IT'S ALL RIGHT TO HAVE BUTTERFLIES
IN YOUR STOMACH.
JUST GET THEM TO FLY IN FORMATION.**

Right now, we bet you could act like the most confident person in the world. Here's proof. Suppose we offered you $1,000,000 if you could act supremely confident for the next 10 minutes. Could you do this? Of course you could!

So here's what we want you to remember:

1. It's okay to be worried. Everybody worries.
2. You can act confident no matter how you feel.

**"ACT THE WAY YOU'D LIKE TO BE,
AND SOON YOU WILL BE
THE WAY YOU ACT."**
— Leonard Cohen

CHAPTER 32

More on How to Build Confidence

Which came first, the chicken or the egg? No one is really quite sure. But what comes first: your feelings or your actions? We know the answer to that one.

Your **actions** create your **attitudes**.
Your **motions** create your **emotions**.
Your **movements** create your **moods**.

In other words, if you start **acting** a certain way — you will start **feeling** a certain way.

If you start acting confident, you will eventually start feeling confident.

If you wait until you start **feeling** confident, you might wait forever. But you can start **acting** confident right now! The more confidence you can build, the better off you will be.

Here are four ways to increase your self-confidence.

1. **Follow the 15-minute rule**. Promise yourself that starting tomorrow, you will do something good within 15 minutes of getting up. Maybe it will be exercising, or eating a nutritious breakfast. Maybe it will be getting to a chore you've been neglecting. Or doing a good deed. By starting your day with the 15-minute rule, you set a pattern of success for the whole day. By keeping this promise, you increase your self-belief.

2. **Set goals and achieve them**. Promise yourself that you will run a mile every day, or finish a project one day ahead of time. And then do it! Every time you set a goal and achieve it, you send a signal to yourself that you have changed in an important way.

3. **Work outside your comfort zone**. The future belongs to those who dare. Nadia Comaneci, the first gymnast in Olympic history to be awarded the perfect score of 10.0, didn't begin her career with Olympic-level skill. She mastered one skill, then tried a harder one. The very act of seeking out new challenges and meeting or exceeding these challenges will make you feel good about yourself.

4. **Make it about others.** Play for something outside of yourself, like your teammates. Be careful of the way you frame this in your mind. Avoid saying, "I don't want to let them down." That will put too much pressure on you. Say instead, "I will help them as much as I can."

5. **Develop rituals.** Golf legend Bobby Jones said that rhythm and confidence are two sides of the same coin. If you're missing one, use the other. What does this mean for you? Do the same things every time when getting ready for a competition. Do them in the same order for the same amount of time. This ritual sends your brain a signal that it is time for peak performance. Hall of Fame baseball player Wade Boggs ate chicken every day, fielded the same number of ground balls during infield practice and ran his wind sprints according to a schedule.

CONFIDENCE IS A MUSCLE. YOU CAN DO SOMETHING TO STRENGTHEN IT EVERY SINGLE DAY.

CHAPTER 33

Are You Too Busy to Read This?

There is one sentence that can destroy your chance to reach your goals. This sentence can also destroy your motivation and ruin all of your relationships. What is this "killer" sentence? You hear it all the time, and you probably say it yourself.

Here's the sentence: "I was too busy."

"I was too busy" seems fairly harmless, but when you use it as a rationalization or an excuse, it can destroy your life. Where does its destructive force come from?

It's OK to be "too busy" for the little things that don't matter. However, there's never an excuse for being "too busy" for the most important things.

One of the best time-management books of all time is "How to Get Control of Your Time and Your Life" by Alan Lakein. We recommend you read it. Former President Bill Clinton did. Lakein's book had such a significant impact on Clinton's life that it's the very first thing he wrote about in his almost 1,000-page autobiography! It tells readers to prioritize their lives into three categories — A, B and C.

A's are the most important things in your life. They are the "must do's." B's are important but not that important. They are the "should do's." C's are of very little importance. They are the "nice to do's."

You can never be too busy for your A's. For example, imagine Yankee superstar Derek Jeter telling his manager, "Sorry I missed last night's game. I was too busy to get to the ballpark because I was watching TV."

If you're too busy for your A's — **YOU'RE TOO BUSY!**

If you're a musician, you have to practice every day. You can never be too busy to practice.

If you're an athlete, you have to practice every day. You can never be too busy to practice.

If you're a student, you have to go to class, take notes and study. You can never be too busy to do these things.

Motivational speaker Jim Rohn says that too many people are "majoring in minor things." Know what your major things are! Don't let your B's and C's interfere with your A's.

YOUR PRIORITIES
DETERMINE
YOUR PROGRESS.

CHAPTER 34

Two Things Your Opponents Won't Do

If you can do two things, you will zoom past 98 percent of your opponents.

Start with this quote from the book "The Only Thing That Matters" by Neale Donald Walsch.

"98 percent of the world's people are spending 98 percent of their time on things that don't matter."

Test that quote against your own life, and see if it isn't true. We regret the past and worry about the future. We think about things like status and comfort. We let things that are **important** crowd out the things that are **vital**. No matter how we try, we can't keep our focus on what really matters.

If you want to zoom past 98 percent of your opponents, you must change this. You must do two things: First, identify what you must do. Second, make sure you do it.

Pick out the one thing that would make the biggest difference in your life. Maybe it's lifting weights more often. Maybe it's studying chemistry with more attention. Or consuming fewer calories.

This idea of **identifying and doing what's essential** comes from Coach Tully's father-in-law, who helped build the navigation system on the first manned spaceship to land on the moon. At the height of the space race, he had a heart attack. The doctor told him to eat an orange every day. Coach Tully's father-in-law took the advice, and ate an orange every day for the next four decades. He regained his health, returned to work and built the navigation system, enabling man to land on the moon — the technological feat of the 20th century! It all happened because the doctor **identified what was important**, and Coach Tully's father-in-law **made sure it got done**.

Football coach Vince Lombardi became a legend with his many championships, including two Super Bowls. There was nothing fancy about Lombardi. He insisted football came down to just two things: blocking and tackling. Guess what he spent most of his time on?

WHAT'S YOUR VERSION OF THE ORANGE? WHAT IS THE ONE THING THAT WOULD MAKE A HUGE DIFFERENCE IN YOUR LIFE?

WILL YOU DO IT?

CAN YOU IDENTIFY THE THING TO DO AND THEN DO IT? YES!

WILL YOU IDENTIFY THE THING TO DO AND THEN DO IT? THAT IS YOUR CHOICE.

CHAPTER 35

Forming the Winning Habit

Vince Lombardi said, "Winning is a habit. Unfortunately, so is losing."

If that's true, you want to develop the winning habit. And **the best way to win is to win**.

There are lots of chances to win every day. Here are three:

The free-time battle: Everyone has some free time. Some people have more than others. Whether you have a lot or a little, make good use of it. Whenever you make good use of your free time, you win.

The nutrition battle: Temptation is everywhere. There's always a choice in what you eat. You can *fill* your body or *fuel* your body. Whenever you make the right nutrition choice, you win.

The most vs. now battle: Can you give up what you want now for what you want most? This is what psychologists call delayed gratification. For example, can you give up hanging out with your friends for working out in the gym? Can you give up wasting time for time spent studying? If what you want *most* beats what you want *now*, you win.

THE MORE BATTLES YOU WIN, THE MORE OF A WINNER YOU BECOME.

CHAPTER 36

The One Skill Where You're a Perfect 10

Suppose you're a basketball player and one day at practice Michael Jordan shows up.

You compete against Jordan on different physical tests. Who do you think would run faster, jump higher and shoot better? Who do you think has quicker reflexes and reaction time? Michael Jordan, right?

Michael Jordan can beat you on all those physical tests. But can you go back to practice and instantly **choose** to have the intensity, the attitude and the effort of a Michael Jordan?

Yes.

That's what's so amazing about psychological skills. They are a choice.

You may not be a pro athlete, but you can act like one. Right now. The choice is up to you.

**INTENSITY,
ATTITUDE
AND EFFORT
ARE A CHOICE.
GET YOURS RIGHT.**

CHAPTER 37

The World's Greatest Motivator

The following story never happened, but it is always happening.

Once upon a time, there was a wise man who traveled from town to town. He would sit in the town square and give people advice on their families or their business or their romantic lives. Every person would give him a few coins for his time.

The wise man was beloved in all but one of the towns he visited. In that one place, there were two brothers who were very jealous of him. Every time he showed up, they tried to make him look like a fool. But they never could because he was so wise.

One night at dinner, one of the brothers said, "The wise man is coming tomorrow, and I finally figured out how to make him look senile."

"What," said the other brother, "are you going to do?"

"I'm going to make sure I'm the first one in line, and when the wise man shows up, I'm going to say, 'Wise man, many people in this town think you have lost your wisdom. To prove your wisdom once and for all, just answer this very simple question.'

"I'm going to put a little butterfly in my hands and put them right in front of the wise man's face.

"I'm going to say, 'Wise man, is this butterfly alive or dead?'"

The other brother protested, "What will that prove? It doesn't make any sense at all."

The scheming brother replied, "You haven't heard the ending. If the wise man says the butterfly is dead, I'm going to show everybody a live butterfly flying away.

"But if the wise man says the butterfly is alive, I'll just press my knuckles together slightly and everyone is going to see a dead butterfly. So no matter what he says, he is going to be wrong."

The brothers couldn't wait until the next morning, and they were first in line when the wise man showed up.

Just as he planned, the one brother said, "Wise man, many people in this town think you have lost your wisdom. To prove your wisdom once and for all, just answer this very simple question. Is this butterfly I have in my hands alive or dead?"

Without a pause, the wise man looked him straight in the eye and said, "The answer is very simple. The answer is in your hands. It's your choice. It's up to you."

And so it is with everything we've talked about in the previous pages. All the information, all the strategies, all the advice. It's all in your hands. It's up to you.

OPPORTUNITIES.
CHOICES.
CONSEQUENCES.

CHAPTER 38

Why You Can Be Great

To sum up, we invite you to look back at the previous pages and see if there's any discussion of your **physical** ability. You won't find any! We don't care how big, strong or fast you are — and neither should you!

There's something much more important than your physical qualities. It's what goes on inside your head. Your future depends on the **thoughts** you think and the **choices** you make. Golfer Bobby Jones said his sport "is played mainly on a five-and-a-half-inch course, the space between your ears."

Here are some thoughts and decisions that will determine whether you become great:

HOW BIG WILL YOU DREAM?

What's your big dream? Climbing Mount Everest? Performing on Broadway? Winning a championship?

There are two guarantees about a big dream:

1. It will be difficult.
2. It will be worth it!

Did you ever see players rush onto the field after winning a championship? They yell, they jump up and down, they hug. You won't hear a champion say, "It feels pretty good to win, but all that work wasn't worth it."

Dream a big dream, then start working to make it reality! Dreaming big *is a decision, and it doesn't matter how big, strong or fast you are.*

HOW WILL YOU REACT TO FAILURE?

Getting what you want isn't easy. You will fail. Failure is guaranteed. It's part of the process. Soichiro Honda, the founder of Honda, said: "Success is 99 percent failure."

But make sure your failures are temporary, not permanent.

Permanent failure = "I can't do it."
Temporary failure = "I can't do it yet."

Bounce back.
Fail. Fail. Fail.
Fail. Fail. Succeed.
Fail. Succeed. Succeed.
Succeed. Succeed. Succeed.

How you react to failure *is a decision, and it doesn't matter how big, strong or fast you are.*

HOW DO YOU VIEW PROBLEMS?

Life is a continuous series of problem-solving events. In most cases, the problem is not the problem — the problem is how you handle the problem. Do you get fascinated or frustrated?

Problems get easier with fascination.

They get more difficult with frustration.

Problems get solved with fascination.

They get worse with frustration.

Fascination brings energy.

Frustration depletes it.

Frustration never works. Fascination always does.

Fascination or frustration: Your choice.

How you view problems *is a decision, and it doesn't matter how big, strong or fast you are.*

WILL YOU REALLY CHANGE?

Everyone knows how hard it is to change. But everyone is WRONG! Change is easy. Smokers have stopped smoking hundreds of times. Dieters have lost tons of weight on diets. But smokers return to smoking and dieters go off their diets.

Changing is easy.

Staying changed is hard.

Your life doesn't come down to practicing once, or eating good meals once, or studying once. Your life comes down to how well you can do it every day. Coach Tully spent years in professional clubhouses, and the word he heard most often was "consistency." Pro athletes try to avoid peaks and valleys. Never too high and never too low. They know that they must grind it out **day after day**, one day at a time.

Whether you stay changed *is a decision, and it doesn't matter how big, strong or fast you are.*

WILL YOU HAVE RESULTS OR REASONS?

There are only two types of people in the world:

Those who do.
Those who don't.

The difference? Those who do — DO! Those who don't — DON'T!

DOers get it done. They bring the ship in. DON'Ters don't get it done. They tell you how rough the seas are.

What do you want? Results or reasons?

Getting results or reasons *is a decision, and it doesn't matter how big, strong or fast you are.*

WILL YOU HOLD BACK OR GO ALL OUT?

You're standing on the high diving board. You've never been there before. You're scared. What are you going to do?

Two choices:

1. Hold your nose and jump in feet first.
2. Go for the spectacular swan dive.

You know the answer: Go for the swan dive! Risk the belly flop. Risk the embarrassment. Here's the ultimate question in life: Are you going to hold back or are you going to go all out?

Movie heroes go all out.
Sport heroes go all out.
War heroes go all out.

No one wins the Medal of Honor by holding back. Be the hero of your own life. Don't hold back — GO ALL OUT. Shock the world!

Going all out *is a decision, and it doesn't matter how big, strong or fast you are.*

ARE YOUR CIRCUMSTANCES TOUGHER THAN YOU ARE, OR ARE YOU TOUGHER THAN YOUR CIRCUMSTANCES?

Dr. Gilbert has a magic book. It's not the Bible, or a dictionary, or his schedule book. It's "The Diving Bell and the Butterfly," a memoir written by Jean-Dominique Bauby. At one time the editor of the fashion magazine *Elle*, Bauby had a life full of travel, glamor and status. Then one day, at age 43, he suffered a massive stroke that left him unable to move any part of his body except his left eyelid.

So how did he write his book? He did it with his therapist by blinking his left eye. The whole project took them more than 200,000 blinks!

Dr. Gilbert keeps this book because it energizes him. It reminds him of Bauby's remarkable victory over circumstances that would have defeated many others.

You, too, can think of this book and ask yourself which is stronger: you or your circumstances.

Rising above your circumstances *is a decision, and it doesn't matter how big, strong or fast you are.*

CAN YOU PUT OFF WHAT YOU WANT *NOW* FOR WHAT YOU WANT *MOST*?

Before wrapping up, we want to touch on this question again because it is so vital to your future.

Choices like this come up all the time:

You'd love to make the team, and your coach has given you a preseason program to follow. It calls for you to run today, but your friends are going to the mall.

Do you go with your friends (what you want **now**), or do you run so you can make the team (what you want **most**)?

People become successful when they act on what they want **most**. They delay the gratification until the work is done.

Putting off what you want now *is a decision, and it doesn't matter how big, strong or fast you are.*

SUMMARY

All these questions add up to incredible news for you. They have nothing to do with your height, strength or speed. They are choices that you can make.

Look at the movie "Rudy," about the Notre Dame football player who worked harder than anyone even though he didn't play in games.

He had a choice every day. He could have moped, missed practice, or quit. Instead, he kept trying. That's why he's famous today. He wasn't a great football player, but he was a great person and a great example for us. His career was a series of correct decisions.

Be like Rudy.

Your success is something you can control. The more often you answer the questions the right way, the more likely you are to achieve what you want.

YOU CAN CHOOSE TO BE GREAT.

If You Like This Book

Want more?

Here are other ways Dr. Gilbert and Coach Tully can help:

Dr. Gilbert's Success Hotline: (973) 743-4690

Coach Tully's blog: totalgameplan.com

Dr. Gilbert and Coach Tully do motivational seminars, phone consultations and team-building sessions. To inquire or to schedule, just email:

Dr. Gilbert sendmeastory@aol.com

Coach Tully edgetully@optonline.net

Dr. Gilbert Twitter: @SuccessHotline

Coach Tully Twitter: @TotalGamePlan

NOTES

NOTES

NOTES

Made in the USA
Charleston, SC
08 April 2014